SHE TOOK OFF
HER WINGS AND SHOES

May Swenson
Poetry Award Series

SHE TOOK OFF HER WINGS AND SHOES

poems by

Suzette Marie Bishop

UTAH STATE UNIVERSITY PRESS
Logan, Utah

Utah State University Press
Logan, Utah 84322-7800

Manufactured in the United States of America
Cover design by Barbara Yale-Read
Cover photograph by Timothy Tracz

"Elegant Shrimp in Champagne Sauce," "Horrorscope," "Visiting Relatives," and
"Emitting a Sound" first appeared in *The Little Magazine*.
"Departing Iceland" first appeared in *The Spoon River Poetry Review*.
"Conversation with Anne Truitt" first appeared in *Aries*.
"House-Sitting" first appeared in *The Antioch Review*.
"One Summer" first appeared in *The Albany Review*.
"Hannah Höch" first appeared in *Fugue*.

Library of Congress Cataloging-in-Publication Data

Bishop, Suzette.
  She took off her wings and shoes : poems / by Suzette Marie Bishop.
    p. cm.
Winner of the 2003 May Swenson Poetry Award
  ISBN 0-87421-567-6
  I. Title.
  PS3552.I77234S54 2003
  811'.6–dc21
                                2003011389

Dedicated to
my husband
RICHARD WRIGHT

CONTENTS

She Took Off Her Wings and Shoes is an extraordinary book. I mean no hype; whoever reads it will, I believe, be blown away by it, as I was. Blown away, or at any rate buffeted, as by a sudden hard wind, of the sort that hits you sideways while you are driving across a bridge, making you somewhat anxious about reaching your destination. Actually, Suzette Bishop's language is itself the bridge, the car, the wind, the dangerous rocking, the ultimate safety.

Technically, Bishop is all over the map. She can do a simple, casual, conversational lyric poem about childhood friendship, or morning light in a seaside bedroom, or reading epitaphs in a graveyard, that looks and sounds like many other poems you've read, only a little fresher, just a little levitated off the page. But her signature work is formally radical, in ways May Swenson would enjoy. Many of her poems are acts of brutal (or tender) linguistic splicing. "Elegant Shrimp in Champagne Sauce" is a three-way braid involving the text of a chic magazine's advice for a dinner party, memories of shifting rented rooms with a beloved and indigent mother, and a present-tense dream meeting with that mother. "Exit Interview" splices the smarmy scripted voice of a corporation flack with the writer's unspoken responses. "Wedding Triptych" wickedly juxtaposes advice from one of those horrible wedding manuals designed to help you spend scads of money ("A good professional videographer, unlike a relative or other amateur, will be prepared for the unexpected and have the skills to add artistic touches") with the reality ("A no spitting sign hangs above the front door of City Hall"). Now there's an artistic touch! Does one laugh or cry? Yes, and the variant typefaces are part of the fun, part of the pain.

Like many poets today and always, Bishop makes art out of her life: the family story, the love story, the personal journey. She also dives into other lives. There is a brilliant sequence of poems re-creating the journeys and sensibilities of women artists like Eva Hesse, Sor Juana Inés de la Cruz, and Christina Rossetti. Here the splicings are from the artist's own writings, and the poems are alternately heartbreaking and triumphant. And then there is the long title poem that ends the book, a meandering meditation on the goddess Fortune, that possesses a troubling grace, with its seemingly aleatic construction that so well embodies chance as an aesthetic as well as biographical rule. Where are we in this poem? What time is it? Here, there, skipping years, looping, longing, losing, surviving, closing with a heron that "flies beside me effortlessly" like an image of achieved poetry.

Wild, bold, furious, generous, unsubdued, hilariously and painfully dishing up our world in chunks of cognitive dissonance that mysteriously evolve into something lovely, *She Took Off Her Wings and Shoes* is deeply personal, extravagantly public art. I was thrilled to read it.

Alicia Ostriker

ONE

Do Not Drive into Smoke

REACHING FOR YOUR HAIR

I lay on my cousin's bed covered by a white cotton bedspread,
its skirt filling with the salty wind and the morning light
allowed to pass through wearing lace veils.
The clock's face is shaped like a boat, and it skims glass waves.

My cousin used to pull my hair, taking it deftly in her fist
and yanking, the blond lengths a light shut out.

One night, she showed me a photograph
of her older sister who died before we were born.

That summer, I hid deeply among the reeds where
no one could find me, their voices pulled into the lengthening
    shadows.
All I could hear were the reeds, whispering strands of hair.

Here I am, your sister ghost, geese sifting up toward the sky,
their full-throated calls unveiled
and carried by glass waves, my hand reaching for your hair.

DISRUPTIONS

From the back of the school bus
Steve threw the box of chocolates
so that it landed squarely
in Kristin's lap.
A perfect aim.

When we turned around,
he was looking nonchalantly
out the window.
Kristin began opening the paper bag
and exclaiming over the heart-shaped box.

Nothing more flew between
Kristin and Steve—
they went to one movie
and that was all.
Kristin and I

went back to our board games
and bicycle rides
in the afternoons.
Her hair streamed out behind her,
and I took it up like a train.

I got the chocolates Kristin didn't want,
the ones she smashed,
their cherry and lemon fillings oozing out.
I got the paper shells.
I got to throw out the emptying, soaring heart.

ELEGANT SHRIMP IN CHAMPAGNE SAUCE

You're sitting outside the French doors.   *It's night and I'm startled to see you sitting there on a stone bench. I see your profile in the dark.*
When you want to have friends over, but don't want to spend all day getting ready, this simple but elegant dinner is perfect.
Your face is sad; you are like a stone statue outside my lighted house.
I think the last place we had our furniture was at the house where you lived as a companion for an elderly woman.   We put our things in the garage.   We lived among the woman's objects. I keep wondering if our furniture is still there.   You left it there.

Chill the champagne and fix dessert first.   We came back to the house to see if we'd forgotten anything.   We left the piano and my dollhouse that time.   *I'm coming out of a twenty-first-century apartment.   There are many apartments like this—low, near the ground, level, with sloping roofs, lanterns set into the stairs.*

I woke up screaming for sleeping pills when I was sleeping on a cot in our empty kitchen. I was twelve that summer, the stairwells were filling with huge moths.   I could hear them flying through the stairwell.

While cooking liquid for shrimp is reducing, start grilling the vegetables.   The landlady came to talk to you about the back rent. I stayed in the bedroom like you told me to. You and she had coffee and talked quietly.   The sheriff came a month later.   The next time, there were fists pounding on the heavy door for a while, and they were going to break it down. We had our things put in storage in the night and stayed at a neighbor's.

They were very gentle women with large, sad eyes and all starving. They had long, bony arms. They shared their breakfast with us.
Reheat shrimp and mushrooms in sauce just before pasta is done.

The sky is empty and colorless. There are lawns, but few trees or shrubs. Lanterns set near the ground along drives and sidewalks are the only beautiful things.   We stayed for a while at a relative's house. They lived in an arboretum. The bay, exotic birds, and trees

[5]

surrounded us. I slept on an army cot. Everyone thought I would like sharing my cousin's room, the lace curtains, frilly girl's bedding, shells, earrings, closet full of girl's clothing, dolls, porcelain animals, her white furniture with gold trim "just like" my furniture.   When I was in the room by myself, I could almost pretend it was my own room, but when my cousin was there, it became hers again. I spent hours riding my bike along the trails during the warm fall, the trees making a shelter above me with their interwoven boughs.

To make dessert, peel four (preferably seedless) oranges, removing as much of the white pith as possible. Slice oranges into "wheels," put them in a shallow serving bowl, and toss with a few tablespoons of Grand Marnier and a teaspoon or so of sugar, if needed. They're great accompanied by really decadent chocolate truffles.

We had our things again in our new apartment.   But the eviction notices and bill collectors began coming again.   The new place we moved to was rundown, and the neighbors kept a wild dog in a cage near their property line to guard it. They never let the dog out. We went over to introduce ourselves when they were having a yard sale. The mother kept her children near her and had a tight, very polite smile.   My room was lavender.

Sometimes the heat shut off in the middle of the night, and my mother would go outside in the cold in her nightgown to go down to the basement to switch the furnace back on.   And my mother heated water on the stove so that I could wash my hair. There were ants in the kitchen cupboards, and they poured out of a box of cereal when I was pouring out a bowl for breakfast. I threw it on the floor and ran to school.

Sauté mushrooms in a medium saucepan in hot olive oil over medium-high heat. Cook just long enough to release mushroom juices and let them evaporate.   *I want to stay in the apartment that's already furnished with white swiss-dotted sheer curtains, afghans, handmade quilts, a brown couch, and bay windows.   I don't want to leave these things. As I live there, I become attached to the apartment, its rooms.   The houses along my walk to the bank remind me of the neighborhood where I grew up—low, small ranch houses.   I realize* *they had looked much bigger when I was a child. Now, they seem very small, like dollhouses, and the neighborhood is empty.   All the girls are in their nightgowns   wandering through the woods with candles.*

The roommate who is incredulous I haven't contributed an equal number of appliances, cookware, and furniture to the apartment. I want to tell her these were all taken from me and give her an inventory of what I used to have.   *I am floating past neat, suburban houses, small ones with little flowers planted out front. One of these is our old house.   The landscape opens up   to fields, green fields.*

Remember the small kerosene lamp made of white porcelain with roses on it, the blue china, painted with people   gathering hay at harvest time.

MY DREAM HOUSE

You fix something at the stove,
the wallpaper peels above the sink,
and most of the windowpanes are broken.

I've been away awhile,
but you aren't surprised to see me
as you lead me to my old bedroom.

You place a quilt and pillow
on the end of the stripped mattress.
From the window I see the backyard

filled with old cars
junked and left to rust.
An Oldsmobile lies on its side

trenched into the ground.
It is a classic with backfins,
the one in a photograph

of you with dad.
You wear red lipstick,
and your hair is black.

Before the June day ends,
we sit on the back stoop
and eat chicken you made.

At the edge of the yard
each tree sharpens and begins to dissolve—
you'll be driving through a night without stars.

HOUSE-SITTING

I step over the golden retriever
lying on the curved staircase.
She looks up at me,
the golden color faded around her eyes
in white rings.

Her owner's eyes are the same soft brown.
I noticed them
as she told me how to use the microwave oven
and about taking in the newspapers.

Her young eyes are in the photograph on the dresser
turned toward her husband's face,
in a later photograph she stands next to him
looking into the room.

And they are in her son and daughter's faces,
Alice wearing a black prom dress
which makes them deepen into pools.

The dining room is taking on an orange glow,
and the plants begin to lean toward the last light
which pulls them into shadows
more encompassing than their clay pots.

I avoid shutting out the lights
and ascending the stairs,
hearing the daughter's many earrings
shake on her dresser

until I lie in the large, empty bed
beneath the down quilt,
so light I can hardly feel it,
or the animal curled against my spine.

KNOWING OBJECTS WILL OUTLAST THEM

It is familiar to her
that the sharp scent of the apples
she places in a turquoise bowl
wavers throughout the house.

Incised fish swim around
the outside of the bowl.
She follows their perpetual circles,
remembering the speckled shells
lying in the tray nearby,
just washed ashore.

Pushed out by the cactus plant,
the waxy blooms are expected
like tiny stillbirths.

She stands in the stairwell
taken into the ink landscape,
the ashes and holly
taking into themselves
the winter twilight.

The ancient stone pipe
lies glued together on the shelf.
The hands that held it
attempted to leave
unforgettable strokings
along the carved moon and its rays.

MY GOWN IS A MOMENTARY OUTLINE

I arrive rain soaked to talk about subletting for the summer.
The two women who live here are getting ready for a ball.

One woman bends over in her slip as she irons her white lace gown,
her cheeks reddening from the steam.

The other woman arranges her hair at a mirror.
She is cocooned in sky-blue silk.

A friend arrives wearing a ruby gown,
and we all exclaim over the dress. One woman's face begins to fall.

For a summer I will have a fireplace, a dishwasher, a swimming pool.
I barely use them. I find myself pulling the draperies apart

and standing on the terrace as daily thunderstorms pass.
With the first rainfall, steam rises from the burning pavement.

My gown is made from the same meeting of cold and heat.
My gown spills like rain and is windswept,

The color of the leaves turned inside out before the sky cracks open.

DRAGONS

I steal orchids during the night,
bending to loosen them from their sisters.

They are rustling, bleeding a little
into my cool palms,

a milk-white blood.
In the house they are burning the memory

of another gathering you closer
with poppy and hibiscus.

The orchids' scent reaches into my sleep
like the wrought-iron tongues of two dragons

flanking the suburban gate.
I choose the black vase decorated with dragons

to surround me like a fiercely carved night.

THE BAT

You arrive again with your leathery wings
stretched over the first autumn winds,
to sleep in my skirts.

You watch me out of the corner of your eye
and reel toward me,
brushing my face without a sound.

You fly around the room
with your scalloped wings,
then cling to the wall upside down.

I let you sleep there and fly out the window
toward high-pitched sounds
like tiny shrieks.

You wait for me,
folded together, a small shield
against lamplight and intimacy.

ONE SUMMER

With the laundry machines, we spin and whir through the afternoon
small, inessential—braided girls, boys in torn shirts, babies crying.
Women smoke as they fold hot clothes,
a bone-thin attendant wipes down the machines.

I stay until my gaze is pulled from the concrete floor
and orange plastic chairs to the heavily vined streets,
to the ashes beginning to fill with nightfall.
I carry a sack of clothes along the honeysuckle-lined roads
empty of young students.
I let the rain cool my sweating back and legs.

Nothing ever touches me during the days of that summer
as I type forms in a basement office, windowless.
I spend the summer nights alone.
The woman upstairs passes over the floorboards hourly
to her crying child. I finish a paper for school
on *A Midsummer Night's Dream*, writing at night
beneath the hurricane lamp, serge-blue curtains drawn between me
and the awakened cicadas, skunk, possum.

A few times a man visits me in the kitchen.
I lean back in the rocking chair.
One night he leaves then returns an hour later
during a fierce thunderstorm knocking out the lights.
I let him into the house. I am holding a candle.
We make love, and rain-filled air cools our bodies. And he leaves.

I wake to find the living room ceiling caved in,
the plaster covering everything.
I stand among the ghostly shapes of furniture.

EXIT INTERVIEW

You haven't liked what you've been doing, have you?
I stayed near the corner windows of the office, the cockpit of a plane facing the Blue Ridge.

But your employment with us has been mostly a positive experience for you, hasn't it?
The last day home from work I see a girl with long black hair, dancing in a field.

You really want to be doing something else.
I want the dusk light falling in sheets. I want to gather the blue between the stars at the point of turning black.

It will all be a distant memory.
I shut the car door, putting it between us. He drives off into the distance.

You need to be tougher.
Have you seen the turtle's shell, cracked and broken?

You'll be doing what you want now, so think about that instead.
I see the ocean, celadon like his eyes, a horizon line, so many whitecaps.

Did they know you'd be leaving so soon?
I slipped through their fingers, leaving my skin, the copper scales dried and falling apart in their hands.

MELINDA

I don't think there will be another day
like that day we drove in your truck
to the edge of the Hudson River
near a bike path and sat on the hood
with a six-pack of beer until
the dusk slipped into the river,
and tugboats passed us, their lights
flashing, reflected on the water.

We were just talking about nothing,
just quietly watching the river and air.
I haven't had that kind of ease
with a friend since then.
Your sculptures are gone from the apartment,
too, a blue-green coffee table
with a wooden shoe glued to the top,
a note in the drawer scolding me
for opening the drawer to look inside,
or your matching bookcase with hands
poking out of the sides, praying.
Your prints making fun of travel posters
lined the walls of a coffee shop
we went to with another friend.

I still have the rock collection you left,
a stone tool rubbed to a point
and smoothed, fossils of insects,
eggs, shells in the other rocks,
what nature welded into those rocks.

Are you sleeping in the bed with a blue-green canopy,
insect netting draped around you,
dreaming of uncut stone, wood,
waves crashing on the beach outside your room?

HORRORSCOPE

Those exacting standards of yours can be ruinous to romance.
I loosen the reins until my hand lets go and lies on his quivering neck. I can be thrown anytime, my foot caught in the stirrup.

Be patient with him, as he must shed prior entanglements. He's worth the wait!
I fish while I wait, letting the fish go after I catch them. A few get tangled in the lines, their gills gasping for water.

In August, an unexpected windfall enables you to make a major purchase, the summer house, condo, or sports car you've longed for.
I'll take the sports car. It will be red, and I'll drive it while I wait, the wind tangling my hair.

A sophisticate's glamour look begins with thick, lustrous hair, restrained by day in a neat French plait, cascading in curls for evening splendor.
I give some of it away hidden in lockets. My heart-strings.

Learn to manage a curling iron for instant perk-ups.
I was wondering what else to do while I wait.

You are <u>driven</u> by a passion for things collectible all year.
The ocean, those shadows, what I see in a child's eyes.

The warm months find you <u>haunting</u> tag sales and thrift shops.
I've returned, sweeping into the stores, hovering above an antique dresser. Can you see me in its dusty mirror?

Marriage is a definite option now—one that may have to be weighted against the possibility of following your career to a distant city.
I stay here in the mirror, neither bride nor professional.

Magic color: periwinkle.
In this color I turn into a shell, a pebble, a stripe on an angelfish fin.

In spring, a body-conscious coatdress in crisp checkered gabardine—accessorize it with bold silver beads. Splashy tropical flowers brighten a flowery strapless mini for summertime frolics.

Deep violet wool jersey draped artfully makes for day-to-evening elegance through fall.

And for winter, a dress like ice floes on the river, that frozen blue color, a belt black-as-night, snowflake earrings.

Much as you'd like to escape to a quiet country inn with him, romance must be put on hold while duty—and destiny—calls.

It's back to hovering white as a bride, the page, snow.

GRAVEYARD

One epitaph cries—*I want to be an angel!*

I see her like one of Leonardo da Vinci's angels
watching from the stand of willows,
her eyes full of evening light.

The names repeat themselves—
Brookes, Woods, Waytes.

We form sentences with their names—
Waiting beside the brook in the woods.
They have waited all their lives
to become brooks and woods,
their true selves.

Another claims—*Just sleeping.*

I see him wake and rise
to follow the road.

The angel awaits his return.

We fall through a grave
sunken from flooding.

One epitaph tells us—*They are not dead.*

See, they stand quietly in nineteenth-century dress,
their eyes hold the evening light
as they speak our names into the grave.

VISITING RELATIVES

The train passes different colored sailboats on the river. Some are
arranged together, some stand alone beneath steep overhanging
cliffs.   My nephew hides behind my sister's legs when I go to
meet them.   He comes down the stairs after a bath, his hair
parted on the side. His younger brother barely notices us and
only cries out for the essentials.   When I catch his eyes,
he giggles.

The woman sitting next to me on the train holds a small radio to
her ear.   I hear the announcer droning on and on.
Light   through the windows at Grand Central Station,
we glide right over the river.

Eddies and pools spread outward.   Cutouts of
moviestars are propped up at the video store.   I watch *Lady
and the Tramp* with my nephew.   Part of a castle rises out of the
small island.   Bases of its ruined moat surround it.   Water
pools out on the bathroom floor at the train station.   Trains'
departures and arrivals flash up on the screen,   letters flip up
onto the screen or disappear behind blinds.

My sister tells me she had an abortion and will be going for a
follow-up visit.   What was missing,   the dog with half her
face white, the other half black,   the jade-colored bird who sat
on my sister's shoulder and flew through her hair.   The worst
part, she said, was waiting in line all day and being last.

My brother-in-law takes food off his son's plate, and his son gets
out of his chair furiously.   He holds the flashing gun in my
face.   The rented video tells the story of a girl raped in a bar.
The men pin her against a pinball machine and fuck her.   My
nephew and I watch Wile E. Coyote chase the Road Runner.
It feels right to be running from the taxi to my house in a
thunderstorm.   Sewage treatment plants, the Bronx, cliffs
border the river.   My brother-in-law spins his son around until
he goes from crying to laughing.

My sister drives us from the train station across Jersey flats, past
Wawas, farmlands.   He holds his head back after a spoonful of

food and gurgles.   The red-haired girl sleeps on the train, a
book held in her hands. The ballerina dances by leaping through
the mirror.   A piece of the mirror juts out of her abdomen.

My nephew's hand rests in mine at the store.   We practice
pressing our faces up against the netting of the playpen to make
faces. He comes running out of the bathroom with his pants
down and stops dinner conversation.   In the home video of
my sister taking the baby home from the hospital, she strokes his
face over and over, her back to the camera.   I stroke his
blond/red hair, his/her/my brown eyes look back at me. He rec-
ognizes himself in the videos.   He says good-bye cheerfully.
The Hudson is full of summer as it carves the rocks.

MIRROR AND SWORD TRICK

Buy something for yourself
for a change,
my stepmother tells my father
something very expensive,
extravagant
like the four-hundred-dollar
mirror she bought,
swimming pool blue,
two palm trees carved
on each side,
or the bamboo furniture
she had flown in from Japan.

My father bought a sword
that was stolen a month later.
I never saw it,
but he said it was silver
with a carved silver sheath.
I imagine engravings of men fighting,
swords raised, clashing
in fiery swirls.

A heavy weapon
he had to hold with both hands,
his fingers wrapped around the handle
in admiration.
Did he try it on?
Admire himself wearing it
in the mirror?
Does he miss the heaviness
of silver?

One of my father's brothers
was shot down during World War II
in his plane,
another brother, useless, lived at home
his whole life,

the third brother, an alcoholic,
called drunk all the time
in the middle of the night,
last year, a suicide in his sixties.

All four brothers trapped,
one in his crashing plane,
one in the house where he was born,
one in a glass,
my father with this woman
who orders him around,
arranging every part of his life,
filling his house to the ceiling
with knickknacks, jars
in the shapes of a figurehead,
a bunch of grapes, a swordfish,
ceramic animals,
and the sword he could
            have used to smash

                        everything   slashing
                  through the bamboo furniture
                              escaping through

      the crack in the mirror   between   the palm
trees

            out into the swampland around him,
vanished.

IN THE HOLY SPIRIT RESEARCH CENTER
Oral Roberts University, Tulsa, Oklahoma

I have avoided coming here as long as I can.
I am looking up citations
for a student's paper on salvation.
Is it my salvation to be
in this circular library,
a white spiral staircase rising up,
up the center to heaven?

I take this staircase to the top floor,
avoiding the guards, since I'm not a member.
I find the room where the Holy Spirit is researched.
Is it here, hovering above the oak table
in this windowless room?
Or in the flame that burns
continuously in a giant torch
outside the building?

At the community college, one of my students
writes about the immorality of wearing jeans,
another that the New Age Movement is a satanic act,
another argues that rock lyrics are immoral.
There is always silence when I ask a question.

The River of Life that winds
through the campus is nearly dry,
and all the gold buildings, skyscrapers,
and giant prayer hands
gleam uneasily in the sunset as I leave.
I have parked behind the Mabee Center,
the parking lot nearly empty.
Maybe the rumors about bankruptcy aren't true,
maybe I will get out safely through the gates after all.

LEAST TERNS

I am all eyes as I drive—
eyes in the rearview mirror, eyes looking
out through the windshield,
out the sideview mirror.
The ice encases me in the car
and makes the car rattle.
I have somewhere to go
and must be there at a certain time,
but this is not where I want to go.
I want to look toward the river
and see the way the light plays
on the water, but I have to keep
my eyes on the road,
and someone is right behind me.

I am having to see from
the corner of my eyes, not fully
anymore, and through tears.
And I am not hearing
the cars passing me,
accelerating, moving efficiently.

I barely heard the doctor
explaining how practical and essential
it would be for me to get a hysterectomy
if I have a third recurrence of abnormal cells.
It would be rolling the dice
if I didn't have one.
It made sense to give up my uterus.

But driving the car along the river
it doesn't matter how much sense it makes,
the trees clinging to the banks,
the least terns ahead of me
then flying over the river,
a whiteness against the black rocks.

BLOODSTONE

We are walking through the rose gardens.
The tall woman jokingly says
another woman at work asked about my fiancé,
the tall woman told her
she would have to wait
since the tall woman was next in line after me.

The sky had been perfect—a powdery blue,
and the roses were at their peak,
but I hear a sucking sound
like a vacuum turned on.
This is how it will be,
at first walking together, easily,
then some turn or words,
and I will be cornered into playing
the jealous woman.
And worse, I am barely seeing the pond,
my face a calm surface,
unable to lose myself in the woods
as the tall woman happily greets
everyone we pass.

Who would have thought
you would find a terraced rose garden
in the middle of the plains?
A garden filled with so many
varieties and colors of roses?
Pink, yellow, white, deep red,
all layered like a cake,
fountains with large goldfish
sliding under lily pads,
tall, sculpted shrubs
and triangular shrubs, their skirts
whipped by the prairie wind.
I was almost somewhere else,
in some other time.

And the greenhouse was even more perfect,
closed into glass.
I almost believe
I'm not closed in with the violet blooms
of the heliotrope opening wide,
the perfume with nowhere to go,
and the spiny cacti aiming
themselves at the sun.

WATER MOCCASIN

When you come in from running
and tell me you saw a large water moccasin
wrapped around a tree trunk
I keep imagining the worst:
I am on my bike and the snake slithers
across the path in front of me,
swirling and twirling its body.
I have to stop, cotton blowing
in slow motion into my face and neck,
the snake's cotton mouth wide open
as it lunges toward me
and bites me just above the ankle.
Or, I come upon the snake
as I walk my bike
across the grass to the road,
its head rears up suddenly.
Or, you can't run past it
fast enough, and it unwraps
itself quickly and drops from the tree,
a wriggling tree root at your feet.

I have to think differently,
more like the archeologist
you told me about who befriends
poisonous snakes at digs,
hanging them from her neck,
letting them sleep in her purse.

It's ninety degrees and barely windy,
the colors of wildflowers are rushing by me,
lavender, reddish-orange poppies,
the bridal-veil lace of Queen Anne's lace,
the white-lined tail of a scissortail
slicing air thermals.
Even this venomous snake fits wordlessly
wrapped around a tree trunk.
It might be fearful of all these people

running, walking, riding bikes, rollerblading,
so it tightly hugs the tree,
and it is less frightening than the man
who asks me for a ride,
or the boys who try to make me wince
by almost crashing into me,
or the women who block my way.

Maybe it's oblivious, even sleeping,
knowing the tree by curving itself
around the tree,
liking the feeling of rough, hot bark
against its belly, its belly
always against something,
against the cool prairie grasses,
sliding through the river water,
moccasin skin touching, feeling, brushing
the earth, the river bottom, the currents
until what is inside the skin
soundlessly slips away.

ANASAZI BOWL

Crates of forgotten artifacts surround you in the museum
    attic.
You hear your breath move in and out of your asbestos mask,
what the men heard who wore masks of animal gods.

You examine an Anasazi bowl, remembering it in your hands,
its perfect round shape emptied.
Before painting, mothers gather together
dirt, stones, petals to make dyes of ochre, red, and brown.
The newly married women ingest soft clay.

Feathered serpents are gods who must negotiate sky and
    earth,
riding the winds blown from sea to slip beneath the fields.

Centuries of earth cover your hands, you see fringes of
    wings in the rain.

DO NOT DRIVE INTO SMOKE

Spiro Mounds, Spiro, Oklahoma
The title of the poem comes from a sign
posted at the Oklahoma border.

We retrace the village at Spiro Mounds,

> as we move along the paths,
> the mounds rise above us
> three mounds together, tiered.

No one lives here now,

the Arkansas River is out of sight,
> but we can hear the barges moving up and down.

Living close to the burial grounds and being buried here
means you have some connection with royalty,

> gods.

The small lodge that held fifteen people
> used smoke to keep insects and rodents away.

Conch shells that may have come from as far as Florida
> are incised with drawings of armadillos.

As we drive away, not even a shape yet
only wisps shifting toward the white sun
> then becoming two deer for an instant

leaping over the highway

then gone,

> not needing to become

anything.

WEDDING TRIPTYCH

I
WEDDING

Finding the right videographer is crucial: should anything go wrong, you won't be able to replay your wedding. There is nothing ceremonious. You are holding an umbrella over me. **A good professional videographer, unlike a relative or other amateur, will be prepared for the unexpected, have the proper equipment, and have the skills to add artistic touches to the ceremony.** A "no spitting" sign hangs above the front door of City Hall. One of the witnesses, Debra, turns on the radio to listen to the weather reports.

Look under "Video Production Services" or "Wedding Supplies & Services." You were smiling down at me intensely. **You'll also have the opportunity to view demo tapes, perhaps even videos of real weddings.** We cross the border into Kansas. You can't get a civil ceremony in Oklahoma. **Your mother, his mother, and your attendants can tell those who ask, where you're registered.** The judge is wearing a Mickey Mouse tie. **A maid of honor is single, a matron of honor is married.** I hold the flowers Debra gave me in my hands—daisies and carnations. **She is expected to assist the bride whenever possible—helping to address the invitations, recording and displaying wedding gifts.** The gold ring is light around my finger. It fits just right. The ring was given to us by a friend of my husband who had gotten divorced. **She also passes the groom's ring to the bride, stands next to the groom in the receiving line, and sits to his left at the bride's table.** We don't have a ring for you, yet.

It is raining. **Editing techniques and special effects (such as adding the names of the wedding party as "cast credits") will also add to the total cost. If your budget permits, plan to have two cameras cover the ceremony—for the best angles. Ask if the** videographer can mix the two camera sources with soft dissolves (fades between the two cameras), instead of just straight cuts. The video will flow better and have a dreamy effect.   The time before crossing the border. The time returning to the other side of the border and wearing a ring.

Note the quality of the audio. Are you able to hear the bride and groom exchange vows?   Clouds sift through each other. **A videographer shouldn't hesitate to put verbal promises in writing.**   The Cadillac seats are soft, there are reading lamps over our heads, the car hums on cruise control as Debra drives over the prairies, and you are asleep next to me.

II
RECEPTION

Send guests home with a part of your heart.

Candlelight in the afternoon and people standing.

Thank them with favors rich in symbolism, not in cost.

Almonds coated in sugar represent the vow, "for better or for worse."

Candles on the mantle.

Spice cookies bearing wheat sheaves—symbols of fertility.

Romance is in the air with fans, great for summer garden weddings.

Handwrite romantic words on pretty papers, then pleat.

Staple bottom, add ribbon.

Candles on end tables.

From the sea of love: porcelain starfish.

Minicakes make sweet memories, romantic dreams . . .

Altar light.

Altered light.

Then, poppyseed cake with champagne.

III
HONEYMOON

The sky would light up for a moment with heat lightning. It was completely dark on either side of the road, and there weren't any other cars on the highway.   **Shapers are now made with pretty Lycra stretch-lace and are as effective as the old-time rubber girdles.**

The rocks slope steeply below us into a canyon. It is a crater, and the rock walls are purple, rose, silver, and red. Rain showers fall in a gray curtain to the west of us; a buck leaps away into the sagebrush.   In the Petrified Forest the land is pared back to its essential parts—rocks, few trees, few people, canyons, fallen sections of ancient petrified trees. You turn your clocks back here. This place is barren and old as the moon, a curtain of rain, a veil.

After determining what kind of dress you want and where you need control, try on shapers.   We wind down the narrow stairs into the canyon, cliff dwellings arranged like shelves on the steep rocks. I can fit into the small doorways. Soot from fires covers the back walls, and everything that is spoken echoes around and around the rocks that circle us.

Headpieces, which are much more elaborate than they have been in past years, can be a wonderful focal point, according to Irene Farina.   This part of New Mexico used to be a sea. The wall of rock that runs east to west was under water. I imagine coral, fish, algae, sea plants. We are driving on the bottom of a dead sea.   **Veils are being made longer—some are three yards—so that they fall over the train.**

You point to hills that were trading sites.   We stand on what used to be a village. Pottery sherds cover the ground. It's impossible not to step on them. The pliant designs and colors of the paint are still clear. All these fragments of pots from one house are intermixed with fragments from other houses. Rock foundations of houses and circular cooking areas are still here. Below us, the river is barely a trickle, and there is quicksand. Dinosaur bones are being brought up from the mud. **They're being edged with embroidery, trimmed with clear crystal, bugle beads, pearls—sometimes sewn onto the tulle in patterns.**

Ocean—a deep, dark blue with emerald edges along the beaches. We sit on jutting rocks and watch for whale tails to rise from the water. Seals lie on their backs and break mussels open on their chests. Cypresses twist their frail bodies. The air is soft and full of the smell of eucalyptus.

For simple dresses without beading, we use fabric from the dress to create elaborate bows, flowers, and then incorporate them into the headpiece. Brides are also choosing regal tiaras of crystal, pearls, with detachable veils. The red, red, clay-red rocks of Sedona and winding down to them from the pine forest. It is raining and sunny at the same time—a man holding an umbrella looks very small beneath the tall pines, beneath the tall mountain of rock. The rocks are shining from the rain. When we look down the mountain, the shining road weaves like a ribbon as it circles down the steep slopes. We bring back your Mexican silver ring with us that your parents gave us, which your father never wears. It is etched with zigzag markings.

COOL WAGONS & BONE CHANDELIERS

At the Church of Santa Maria della Concezione, Rome

After a fourteen-hour flight over the ocean,
I'm suddenly in a place
where I don't understand anything
anyone is saying
as we wait in the customs line.
And then in the subterranean part
of the airport, we watch the conveyer belts
turning around and around without our bags.
I don't think I thought
to put a pair of clean underwear
or toothbrush in my backpack.

Our friend comes to pick us up,
the taxi races to Rome at over 100mph,
I hang on, the landscape a blur,
the hot wind rushing in through the windows.

The first place he takes us after lunch,
and after a maze of narrow streets, is a church.
At first, I can't see
as my eyes adjust to the dark interior
after the full sunshine outside.
What I notice first is the dank smell,
like dirty laundry.
I thought it was just the smell of an old
stone building, crowded in mid-July.
But antleresque decorations and chandeliers
become clearer, focused, made of bones,
cupping the candlelight,
the bones of the monks who lived here.

Dinner is several courses.
I don't remember the dessert,
something very rich.
The mirrored dining room is still hot
even though there is an air conditioner

in the window, called a Cool Wagon.
We take our time filling out,
pushing further away
from the white tablecloth.

THROUGH THE CORRIDOR

I didn't even know if the fever
was real or if it was just the relentless
heat of Rome in July.

No air conditioning,
the air still and heavy in the room
that looked out on a courtyard

where someone started hammering at six a.m.
from one of the small, fragile balconies.
Even the marble of the bathtub was warm.

I hated feeling sick, weak,
disappointing the maids who were irritated
because they couldn't come in to clean the room,

my husband who wanted to see the sights,
the high ceiling holding in the air,
the dense, green geranium wallpaper waiting.

The owl above the bed *was* real,
its claws grasping its prey,
circles around its eyes,

returning through the jungle in the wallpaper
and finding me there
swimming in the sea among the mare's-tail.

**The EC2001 Panther is a fiber-optic system that transmits informa-
tion over SONET (Synchronous Optical NETwork), video, voice, and
low-speed data.** I wander around and around the gray,
carpeted halls. No one smiles. I must be an invisible signal speed-
ing through a conduit.

**It has a flexible design, a variety of applications, compact size,
software control of customer premise equipment (CPE), and
carries all communications on one system.** He never gets my
voice-mail about leaving work early because my husband is in the
hospital. No one tells him where I am.

**Interactions using Panther include teleconferencing,
videoconferencing, security surveillance, and transmission of data.**
She is telling my boss about all my mistakes. Her long hair is
perfect and falls below her waist. **Fiber-optics involve little
propagation delay.**

I have a project due in an hour, and I am staring at the computer
screen. Snow is sifting through me, covering me, immobilizing
me.

**For instance, with Intelligent Vehicle Highway Systems (IVHS), if an
accident or blockage occurs, remote detectors activate video cam-
eras and relay live video feeds of the occurrence back to the main-
tenance position. Large billboards will then be updated with
messages telling drivers to detour.** At another meeting with
the Personnel Director, he is telling her how inconsiderate I am
and how I can't do my job. His blue eyes are like cursors,
blinking, waiting to be moved. His hair is turning steel gray. How
does the signal know which way to go when it can choose many
different pathways? How does it escape this office where these
descriptions of me are filed away in a personnel file?

**As wireless personal communication services (PCS) become part
of the automobile, messages will automatically display on the
dashboard of the car.** He scolds me about letting my personal
life interfere with my work. I see my husband on the computer
screen, tubes attached to his openings, an incision spanning the

length from his breastbone to below his abdomen. It feels like I'm driving down the wrong side of the street as I drop him off at the hospital and drive on to work.

Thus, lifting either phone will cause the other to ring until it is picked up. Superior analog-signals are achieved, and distortion is minimal. Ethernet can be used in a typical network and bridge different rings together. My husband lies suspended, netted, the center for a network of wires, tubes, a buzz of talking doctors and nurses. For a while I wander the hospital corridors. A scaffolding holds the new wing up outside his room. Some of my husband's friends bring me plants, keep me distracted from the empty, sheeted bed in his room.

Each building will be a separate ring, and the ethernet will act as a bridge so that anyone in one building can talk to anyone in another building. A scope follows the tunneling of his colon, finds the cancerous tissue.

Its blooms are waxy and white against a dark green. The nurses tell me to leave the room, and they close the door while they move him from the gurney to the bed. He is in a lot of pain.

There is no need for separate lines as video, voice, and data are all carried on the same line. The shelf has a backplane which is driven with a control-card that can be redundant. My supervisor goes through the things on my desk when I'm not there. He tells me I can't write. When I do a good job, his mouth tightens, and I wait for the payback, the red marks all over my work, a shorter deadline for the next assignment, time made shorter and shorter.

I am turning to leave the building. I am escorted out on my last day. During the week, the people who used to talk to me pass by me in the hallway as if I'm a stranger. **In addition, the EC2001 accepts either learning-bridge or non-learning- bridge functionality.**

He tells everyone I am a liar. He also tells them that I'm not strong enough. **EC2001 allows CAPS to access the "super information highways" offered by telephone companies.**

Higher bandwidth, like token ring and ethernet, allows for many data protocols at once. I leave when we are in the middle of an air-traffic-control project for an airport in Iceland. I imagine him there, wind and snow whistling past him, his blood turning to ice crystals, his nervous system frozen, shut down, his eyes ice-blue lakes.

My husband awakens from his long sleep, opening his green eyes, and I touch his warm forehead. His warmth shoots up my arm, and my ice-casings crash to the floor.

TWO

As Good There as Here to Burn

AT THE RAMADA INN WITH RUTH AND ESTHER

This poem is based on being a subject in a cold study while writing a research paper comparing Ruth and Esther.

The first night all the subjects feasted together
before we went to our rooms,
a banquet in the garden courtyard,
drinks served in golden goblets,
a sweltering August, hot as the desert.
Afterwards, we were sealed
into our separate chambers,
air-conditioning blowing through.
We were given nose drops before bed.

The next day was mine
in my palace room with white cotton curtains
and blue hangings caught up with cords
of fine linen and purple and silver rings,
marble pillars and couches of gold and silver
on a mosaic carpet with designs
like mother-of-pearl and precious stones.

A virus in a glass bowl
was wheeled into the room on a cart.
I felt fine until the evening,
wearing my robe with its long sleeves,
taking refuge under my feverish wings.

I woke up *before one could recognize another.*
Later, I heard voices outside,
and I parted the curtains,
a group of beauty contestants lay by the pool,
perfect bodies in bathing suits, bikinis,
the men in the cold study
leaned over their balconies.
My eyes were red,
my nose was swollen,
there were circles under my eyes.
She finds favor in his eyes
and is kept close
to the maidens of Boaz in the fields

so as not to be molested.
Beyond the pool, *she gleaned*
the grain, bending and rising up,
widow of the dead.

His anger burned within him,
and he sought beautiful young virgins
so that he could find a replacement
for Queen Vashti.
They were beautified for twelve months,
six months with oil of myrrh
and six months with spices
and ointments for women.
I took a hot bath,
hoping it would stop my aches,
clear my congestion.

Her mother-in-law tells her
to wash and anoint herself
and put on her best clothes
and go down to the threshing floor,
and after she uncovers his feet
he will tell her what to do.
The other twin bed is empty,
and I talk to my boyfriend over the phone.
My throat is sore.

He sets the royal crown on her head
and makes her queen.
But she still risks dying
if she goes before him
when he hasn't called her
and held out the golden scepter to her.

Esther risks this for her people,
Ruth follows her widowed
mother-in-law during a famine,
I eat chocolate cake,
only risking getting a cold,
I get money instead of a crown
or a husband, no banner

draped across my chest
or runway to walk.

By the time we leave
I have an ear infection
and am the one who is the most sick,
no one wanting to come near me.
We ride off in different directions
as if on swift horses
used in the king's service,
bred from the royal stud.

EMITTING A SOUND

Based on the sculpture, journals, and
letters of Christine Woelfle, 1959–1986
Sections in italics are from Woelfle's journal or are titles of works.

Aluminum sends whirring spiral shreds
into my hair, into my mouth, and onto the floor.
I looked up to catch the chance of seeing my daughter,
all the available spaces of her.

Turning from the pine cubes
I open into an unpainted fan,
my spinal column bursting from its shell.
Day passes through me
setting off my gold-leaf curves,
and my rice-paper canopies filter the sunlight
of this plywood summer.
Notice the young pine, my ash-blond hair.

As a child, I ran to hidden places in the woods,
rearranging them
before impending storms.

These rooms, with their emptiness,
their rushing wood floors
will disassemble me.
The body stays claylike, embracing itself.

This weekend the sun was blowing and pushing
as I walked over the sea rocks.
The ceiling of the cathedral is like the spinal cord,
the arches large, leaping waves.

Don't let my stillness fool you.
With my plexiglas skin
I take over the room you've left
and turn into crystal flames.

I felt the sound of every bruised sea urchin
even though I was looking at the debris

[48]

of cracked light collecting itself
on the surfaced underside of the water.

Nothing is more weightless than my house.
Besides a garden,
it reminds me of an Egyptian barge
floating down the Nile, rigged with trellises.

Light drawing on the wall, Persian letters, signatures
are silent constructions.
Everything becomes fluid
even this *Frozen Spring*
I am air dressed in silks and brass jewels,
color that seems to linger too long.

CONVERSATION WITH ANNE TRUITT

Based on Anne Truitt's sculpture and journals

Where are you walking?
A woman is lost in the desert.

Who follows you?
A white rattlesnake, pale as milk. Once it bit me high on the
ankle. I came to know that it intended to stay with me.

Which color are you?
I will myself be ultramarine—from beyond the sea.

Where is your home?
I wish I could live in a lower key in a place like the mobile-home
court through which I walked during a windy desert-smelling
twilight. She feels my work, as I do, to be a kind of home.

Who stands in the doorway?
She is opening her gown with her hand so that she may more
distinctly detect the first pangs of her labor.

What are you listening to?
I seem to hear them now before they become color, as if sound
required color to become visible.

What have you done with the color?
The color is set free into three dimensions.

Are you wounded?
As china is crazed with tiny fissures. It is no wonder that for a year
I have been like a lake of ice under a pale sky. I let the color,
which must have been gathering within me somewhere, stream
down the columns on its own terms.

What is this last turn like?
Behind me the ramparts of blue-black slate rise straight into air
that is only air, not sky, and is itself a blue-black slate. I returned
home, my house alight. This time, I hear the silence the waves
interrupt.

THE CONSERVATOR

She returns the Flemish gown to a redness like the blush
of a shy bride at the threshold of church or house,

falling in perfect symmetrical folds from her body,
released like finely cut rubies from a necklace

and scattered at her feet in dismay.
She cleans years of soot from the lady's pale hands and face,

from the tiled floor in star patterns,
seeing herself reflected in china cups and saucers.

As she wanders this room, the lady's hair moves slightly,
her lips move,

What do you bring me?
She closes her hand over the moth, taking it to the lady;

it flutters in her hand like the eyelids of someone just waking
and flies out the opened door leaving small feathers

on her fingers, in the life-line of her palm.
Ashes, absence of color, the sounds of ships through the opened door.

PURPLE GLOXINIA

Based on a painting by Frances Cohen Gillespie

blossoms   leaves

mirror   table

hang

in   a   blue   space

all the blossoms   are open

flaming   velvety

reflected   in   a   mirror

veined   leaves   inhale

almost   reaching   into

the tablecloth's   world

the dragon   imprinted   on the tablecloth

sends   cranes   flying

in   all   directions

across   the indigo   background

their necks

turned back

to see if he is following them

HANNAH HÖCH

Berlin photomontage artist who used pop images of the Modern woman in her work, 1889-1978
Sections in italics are quotes from Höch's writings or are titles of her works.

My mother was an amateur painter. Eventually four siblings were born. I worked in my father's office, and I was pulled out of the girls' high school to care for this child from the time she was three days old until she was six.   **Hair swept softly off the face is the perfect complement to this season's decidedly romantic turn-of-the-century dresses.**   The night scene in the woods. *Sketch for Memorial to an Important Lace Shirt.*

I studied glass design. I did Red Cross work.   He leaves purple bruises blooming on my arms. I packed up and went to Italy. Much of the trip to Rome I made by foot. The borders had just reopened.   **It's gathered gently high atop the head to expose the sensual taper of the neck, the velvety smoothness of bare shoulders, and to create overall balance.** *(The Painter) Undated, probably 1920. He thought that the treacherous female soul (treachery no doubt its most important element alongside emptiness) could appear as a cubist lemon-yellow spiral among the green.*

Snow and blooms—abortions in January and May. I want to blur the boundaries.   **Keep the look soft, touchable—not lacquered.**   They summoned me to a house on the sea.   He himself was the most perfect Merz work, a continuum.   I met her then. She knew how to put words together, how to look at me.

1933: Hitler. Everyone was suspect. Language was forgotten. We were hermetically sealed off.   Carnivorous plants.   *With Two Faces:* Masks, Veils, Make-up. I keep the edges frayed. **Be careful to choose a headpiece that accents your hairstyle but doesn't overpower it.**

In the Dolomites at an altitude of two thousand meters where I was supposed to recuperate, I met my future husband. We must be open to the beauties of fortuity.   **Your stylist can help analyze your hair's texture and recommend styles that will work with it, not against it.**   A machine that measures beauty.

He disappeared from my life. I've lived alone in a little house with a big garden.

My great loneliness began.   **A haircut is an expression of your-self.**   The woman leaps away from her shadow. She leans in at the hip and then against the air, turning and looking up past her wrist,   past her hand cupping   the shelf's edge.

BENEATH EVA HESSE'S FIBERGLASS VEIL

Visual artist, 1936-1970
Based on Hesse's artwork, her journal, and two biographies.
Sections in italics are quotes from Hesse's journal or titles of works.

I
FROM PAINTER TO SCULPTOR

the positioning

        where it comes from

                        the ceiling

or the floor

Long-stemmed reeds arranged like a forest.   Fleeing Germany.
I studied window dressing.
My mother gone   threw herself out the window,
our cord   snapped apart.

My studio is *less womb-like.* *The glass window from ceiling to floor* in the
old warehouse.   The space in paintings is too flat.   *I find
myself really afraid of the men here at school. They have strange attitudes to
the few women that are around school.*   White-to-gray tendrils
          try to escape their surface.   I thread
            a leadwire   out of the canvas.

I go back to Germany with my husband for a year. My German rela-
tives are all dead.   *Vertiginous Detour.*   Our studios are in an
abandoned factory. All around me: machine parts, joints, nozzles,
rims, wires, hoses.   I start to use them, first papier-mâchéd and
then wrapped with wire and painted to make: penis shapes, circles,
concentric circles, coiled forms, testicles, *C-Clamp Blues,* fragile
crotch, breasts, chairs, lamps, shoes, a vacuum cleaner, penis with
thorns, tendrils, loops, *Two-Handled Orange Keyed Utensil,* umbilical
cords hanging from electric sockets, vagina.

All *ultra alive.*   *My weird humor.*

appears from

                                                    and then

            disappears into the surface

                                    to emerge   again in

another area

At a show of my reliefs and drawings in a greenhouse, some hung
from the rafters *like things growing,* Tom said. My hair was
wrapped into a high beehive, and I was holding a cigarette and
wilting tulips. *I still want to be a little girl,* but no one respects me as
an adult.   *Most others don't know me as an artist.*   *Is it right
for a girl to be a sculpture?*

II
Crazy Grids and Series Not Adding Up

An empty picture frame with just the wire hanger coming into the
room. Fishnet bags netting something with tentacles, pulled out
of the water. *Pink* is made of raised circular forms built up from
papier-mâché, each circle wound in wires, painted pink.

Another relief uses two panels,
wires from one   threaded into   the other
          at precise places,   each tiny wire in its hole,
graceful irregular waves connecting the panels.   He starts to
see someone else. The stress on the panels makes them
                                        both fall.

It ended up in a jungle of strings. Boomerang phallus, gourds made
of balloons plastered over and up in the air. The marriage ends.
My father was in a coffin.

A friend who is a writer gave me a spiral of words to describe me:
*disguised, conceal, wrap-up, cloak, bury, ensconce, hide, entomb, hedge-in,
encirclement, ringed, shell, hull, mummify, shroud, surround, wrap.*
My main tool is a *crudely-shaped wrong side of a brush.*   My
processes are: winding, bandaging, poking through, sewing gone
wild, tying, knotting, wrapping, binding, knitting. I go out further
until lines are pulled out into real space. What's on the back of
something sewed?

Laocoön
A skeletal ladder goes up
rational, reaching up one
rung at a time to a trap door
while wrapped ropes,
snakes,
tangle in the lattices
and pull downward,
everything painted pavement gray,
impressions of my fingers
pressing into the moldings of the ladder.

monochrome entanglements

atrophied organs

private parts
mummified in string.

III
LIVING SPACE

Two sculptors living across the street from my studio masturbate
at their window.   Someone shoots at my back window with a
BB gun. I have two small rooms in my Bowery loft.   I like
working in the living space which is less lonely than my tall-ceiling
studio.   My work table has an ashtray from Persia, a
kaleidoscope, ruler, pencils, a metal spike, pitcher and matching
cup, plastic tubing, and a copy of the periodic table. Fumes from
resin, aluminum wire, papier-mâché, Elmers Glue, turpentine,
polyester resin, Dutch Boy White Diamond Gloss Paint hover in
the rooms and sting my throat.

I pull rubberhose through
the inside of the cube
like hooking a rug. *All
hose goes inward, inside
box; outside box looks
woven* to make a softly
bristling interior.
People at the exhibit
get in it and wreck it.
I collapse the day
I finish re-threading it.

In a glass pastry case I arrange small pieces neatly:

a miniature umbilical cord, shell-cunt, box of string,

sprouting clear tentacles, epoxied sleeves of fiberglass.

I make a box for a friend's son holding a lock of his hair.

IV
HOVERING IN MID-AIR

Fiberglass:

translucent

flexible

ugly

off-white   fleshy

Panels hung like stiff curtains refracting and absorbing light like
windows expanding across the room, passing you in elegant
waves.   I cut off my long hair.   Measurements
disintegrating at both ends, rubberized, loose, open cloth, coarse,
rough, changing, enclosed tightly by glass encasements just
hanging there.   Line connects one impossible space
with another.   Fiberglass poles link the wall to the floor,
and fiberglass icicles hang from the ceiling.   *They are not for
architecture or sun, water or for the trees, and they have nothing to do
with color or nature or making a nice sculpture garden. They are indoor
things.*

Sequel—a continuation of a story or process.   January is the
anniversary of my mother's suicide. My father left her for me.

[59]

SICK: exhaustion, headaches, vomiting, hospital, brain tumor, surgery, radiation, chemo, recurrence.

I draw the windowpanes in a cabin.   It's raining outside.
    The surfaces are opaque but light filled, watery,
        and rectangular shapes float out over the borders,
the window frames.   In a photograph I'm standing behind
    clear cellophane, serious, my arms reaching upward, on
                the other side looking

back.

PHOTOGRAPH OF EDNA ST. VINCENT MILLAY

She is holding a dogwood branch.
          She pulls two branches
     down around her like a screen.

    She is caught in the dogwood branches.
She is small and weightless,
     her head turned.

     All that matters is the dogwood circling around her,
    her eyes seeing
the patterns of gray branches,
        the words opening out into air.

SOR JUANA INÉS DE LA CRUZ

Sor Juana Inés de la Cruz (1648-1695)
The poem is based on her letter, The Answer, *her poems, and the*
painting of her, "Retrato de Sor Juana Inés de la Cruz," painted by
Miguel Cabrera in 1750. Phrases in italics are quotes from poems
and The Answer.

I hold my long necklace of rosary beads
between two fingers.
When I first studied Latin,
I cut off *fingerlengths* of hair.
If I didn't learn all my lessons
by the time it grew back,
I cut my fast-growing hair again.
Hair should not *cover a head*
so bare of facts—
the more desirable adornment.

One long sleeve drapes over
the chair's arm,
and my other hand turns
the pages of a book.
I begged my mother to dress me
in men's clothes.
In these clothes, I saw myself
pacing the corridors of the University.

I slip away and follow my sister
to her lessons.
I lie to the teacher
and tell her my mother wants
me to have lessons, too.
The experience undeceived her.

Books and a clock are behind me.
My writing comes from *a force beyond me.*
Neither the reprimands of others
(for I have received many)
nor my own doubts
stopped me.
My books are my teachers.
Many of them waited for me

on my grandfather's shelves.
I learn from *those lifeless letters*
without a *teacher's voice.*
I am always interrupted.

I gaze directly at the viewer.
Truly, my Lady, at times
I ponder how it is
that a person who achieves high significance
is received as the common enemy.
No one forgives her for the fame she takes away.
Figures of the Winds and of Fame
decorate the highest points of the churches.
To defend them from the birds,
these images are covered with barbs.
Intelligence lacks defense.
I am warned to be more like
other nuns in the convent.

The curve of my rosary echoes
the curve of the table leg,
the folds in my dress.
Some have even sought
to prohibit me from study.
This could be a delusion
of the eye, displaying concavities
where there were none.

I sign in blood
that I will never write again.
I have forgotten the distance
between myself and your most
distinguished person,
which should not occur
were I to see you unveiled.

My hair is tucked away
and hidden by my veil,
my heart undone and passing
through your hands.
Red tablecloth, inkwells, quills

are still as I am in the painting.
Those quills used to *beat the wind*.
And she, rising from fire,
reanimates herself just when
she seems to be consumed.
The morning dew
embroidered her chaste veil with pearls.

I am she who is used
to walk among elegant similes.

THE GHOST OF CHRISTINA ROSSETTI

*This poem is based on Rossetti's poems and biography. Phrases
in italics are from Rossetti's writings and papers.*

My sister warns me not to pick the strawberries until they are ripe
enough. I return to the hedge near my grandfather's cottage. I
watch daily as they grow, reddening, a heavy sweetness I breathe
in. I finger the brittle leaves and seeded skin, but snails eat them
all first.

I learn to wait for what I want, and if it fades before it is mine, I
am better off never having what I want in God's eyes. Fairytales,
nursery rhymes, my nun-sister teach me this lesson, too.   My
brother, Dante Gabriel, takes what he wants without punishment.
I fear for his soul.   I hear both Italian and English,   words
from both languages.   I love the Italian songs my poet-father
sings to us: *Mie care figliuole son fresche viole dischiusse all'albor . . . nel
nido d'amor.*   He fled Naples during a revolt.

Studying Dante, my father loses himself in *The Inferno.* My sister is
the brilliant one but is even better at shutting the doors,
becoming a governess and then a nun. I am able to avoid both
vocations.   William, my oldest brother, is the quiet one, taking
in everything so he can write about us later, always taking care of
us. My mother runs a school when my father can't go out of the
house any more.

I can't avoid nursing my father.   He doesn't know where he is,
and he is going blind.   Alone   with him in the house, he
tells me I look like my mother when she was young. He cries and
yells until I climb into his bed.   I like the way he cups my face
and strokes my hair, quieting, looking at me intensely, *my beloved
papa.*   And I obey when he tells me to unfasten my dress and
lie closer, soothing him,   but I freeze   as his hands move
down me.   I never tell what happens next.

I become good at freezing myself.   But at fourteen when I
can't feel anything, and I know I should be punished for my
secret, I try to break out of my skin, out of the house, cutting my
arms open with my scissors, smashing everything.

How ironic to sit as Mary in her girlhood for my brother's painting. My mother models for St. Anne.   Does she know the secret I keep?   Gold halos circling our faces, my long hair unpinned and falling down my back, innocently. We work an embroidery design together, entangled.   I stare off into the distance, not meeting my mother's eyes or the viewer's eyes. And I am Mary for my brother's painting of the Annunciation. In a white nightgown I crouch in bed as the angel offers me lilies, a dove bursting into the room.   I am ready to leave.   In a woodcut, I am one of many weeping queens in King Arthur's court.   All of us sit in a circle, tears and hair flowing, all of us crowned.

An unfinished portrait by a painter who loves me is truer, a feather painted behind me, my thoughts, my quill pen, my hair pulled back tightly, seriously watching, not sure what is ahead of me, what else my gray eyes will see.   I don't fall in love with him.   But I do fall in love with another painter and, later, a scholar. The painter breaks off our engagement because he loves God more than me. He thinks I understand his calling perfectly, but I let the fire-breathing monsters in my poems speak the truth.

The other man is a *blind buzzard.* We caress each other through our poems.   He takes four years to propose. By then, my feelings, like the waves of the Northern Sea, crash and spend themselves on the beach where I go to recover.   I tell him he isn't religious enough.

I want fame, but I don't tell anyone this. And I don't tell them I write epics instead of the ladies' verses all the reviewers like. My fairytales aren't just for children. Goblins, monsters, crocodiles, ghosts are part of us. Another part of us, a sister, keeps us from our worst selves, from eating rotten fruit.

A prince procrastinates on his journey to save the sleeping princess from near death. He takes all the wrong paths, like my brother.   The princess dies before the prince reaches her with the healing potion.   Is she my brother's wife who died, exhumed from the grave years later when it was too late? Me waiting for a magic kiss, a proposal, a bed I'm afraid to enter? The unattended soul?

I travel to Italy, *Switzerland behind us, we plunged down, all Italy before us*, the mountain slope of St. Gotthard covered in forget-me-nots. *An owl had satisfied my need*, but I never find what I am looking for. In England my burnt-black hair and sun-warmed skin are foreign, and in Italy my snowy manners won't melt away.   *I turn to the bleak North,   the South lies out of reach.*

While my brother visits the riverside pleasure gardens, plucks a streetwalker to take back to his bed, then to his studio to paint, I take the evening watch at St. Mary Magdalene's Home. Prostitutes can find refuge here. Most are young girls living on London's foggy streets, suddenly appearing from the swirling fog in doorways. They are falling, falling, falling.   Tonight, I watch them sleeping, cocooned in warm beds.

Instead of this heart of stone, ice-cold, I want scalding tears.   I lock doors against my moods, but I hear them at the watery coastline, and I catch a glimpse of them, *a pale gleam come and gone as quick as thought, which might be hand or hair.* They draw me out into the cold sea.   While I am gone, I tell everyone I am ill.   My brother is kept in a stone house near the sea.   He is afraid to go out, hears everyone whispering about him, sits in the dark like my father.   Only reading my poems or drawing a portrait of me brings him back.

The girl in my story is chased by Quills, Angles, *whose corners almost cut her*, Hooks, a *scowling Queen.* No one can help the girl. She is tempted by fruits, and as she reaches for them, glowing like lanterns, a glass castle grows around her. When she escapes, she meets an eyeless boy whose mouth is filled with tusks. He wants what she carries in her basket. She will say, "No!" scaring them all away, find her grandmother's house, *the northern lights, each hill as if it smouldered, ready to burst into a volcano.*

Fevers take me.   I can't hold a pen steady, my throat is swollen, my hair falls out, my eyes bulge.   I avoid mirrors. After a year like this, my doctor tells me I have Graves' Disease. I'm not ready to go to my grave. I recover, but I am no longer young.   There are two deaths: my brother and sister. I know Maria flies to heaven. Gabriel does not.   Before he dies, he screams, holding his arms out.   I hope his Beatrice with flaming hair and green dress enters them.

I want to use my fame to help others.   I speak for animals' rights. Many are dissected alive without anesthesia. I do it in memory of an orange tabby cat I ran to after nursing my father. She let me hold her.   I write prayer books, matching saints with English flowers. I'm not allowed to be a preacher, but I can still help you find maternal love from God, better.   And I learn to trust the fatherly God again, his hands reaching out for me.

Unnamed lady, I will speak for you and your sisters, too, fourteen Lady Troubadours, *monna innominata*. My father wrote about Beatrice as the personified secret at the heart of religious worship. I think she is a real person, and I am ancestress to Petrarch's Laura. We become speaking subjects in fourteen sonnets, a sonnet of sonnets.   In these poems, I remember when I first met my love, *half turn to go yet turning stay*.

AS GOOD THERE AS HERE TO BURN

For Lady Mary Wroth

Mary Wroth (1587?-1651?) was the first Englishwoman to write a sonnet sequence (a Crown of Sonnets) and a work of prose fiction. She based the work on the myth of Pamphilia and Amphilanthus, her observations of court life, and her love affair with her cousin, William. Italicized sections are quotes from Wroth's work and have been changed to modern spellings.

The Thread of Love Is the Guide Out

I speak as Pamphilia to Amphilanthus   code-talking
my heart burning.   Only women had to be constant in
love, but Pamphilia tells her lover constancy is an honor for men.
His heat to me is cold.   She saves him from becoming trapped in a
labyrinth and sacrificed to the Minotaur.   He wonders
what he owes her, now.

Childhood — First Turning the Corner

My father goes away to the Netherlands, another world, below,
and to court.   I live with my aunt who is my godmother
from that fire get heat to write.   She teaches me prosody and lets me
loose among the maze of her library.

I read poetry by my father and uncle, my aunt's translations *under night's black mantle.* I run into the room where all the poets are gathered at my aunt's estate. *I offer to your trust this crown, my self.*   I
turn my aunt into the Queen of Naples who was perfect in poetry
and rename her Simena, an anagram for her name.   Mine is
Worth, the way my name is pronounced.   *Still adding fire to burning hearts.*

Dead Ends

My characters' arranged marriages fall apart.   *Such beauty breeds desire.*   My husband leaves me there with nothing but debts,
the thin wraps of other women trailing the ground   *all naked, playing with his wings.*   Our son dies at two, and art does not help
with this grief. *I am long frozen in a sea of ice.*   I write to the King,
begging him to help me out of my debts.   *Who wears Love's Crown, must not do so amiss.*

Amphilanthus can't promise to be faithful to her.   Go to the
heart of the labyrinth.   I belonged to Queen Anne's circle
and played the archlute which is almost as tall as I am.   *Now
willows must I wear.*   I'll dress in the *branches of this tree.*

LOVE — BEWARE OF THE BEE HIVE

My cousin, my Amphilanthus, is married, too, but we meet hidden
by branches *in coldest hopes I freeze, yet burn.*   I carry each of his
two children hidden beneath my full skirts.   Fortune helps
Pamphilia and treats her as a sister, commiserating with her
anguish as a mistress   *like painted outsides.*

Pamphilia saw him and did not see him.   I gaze out from this
painting at William, thinking of him while I am painted, yet I have
to hide what I see except from his eyes.   One way out is
through meeting his eyes,   our secret thread.   Pamphilia
watches the movement of the sun and moon *changing in an instant
space.*

MANY DOORS SHUT

I am charged with slander by a Baron; my poem is mocked in
another Lady's poem.   I am ordered to withdraw my book from
sale.   I   had to leave court circles, *princes: whose thoughts sliding
like swift rivers never rest.*   There is still something left at the
center.   *Let me thinking still be free.*   I will love William
and sign my name to the poem.   Find me like piecing a
mosaic together.   *I but chameleon-like would live and love.*

THREE

She Took Off Her Wings and Shoes

SHE TOOK OFF HER WINGS AND SHOES

Fortune appears in many forms—as the goddess, Fortuna, capricious in her gifts; a slip of paper in a cracked cookie; a roulette wheel in a casino; a pap smear report; an eviction notice; dreams and turns in life recorded in a journal without knowing what will fill the pages that follow.

I
ILL FORTUNE

The chance happening of adverse events, the turns of luck in the course of one's life

Over the phone,   I ask to speak to my mother.   The woman   at the other end of the line   tells me there is no one   there by that name and hangs up.

Living off credit cards.

You seek to shield those you love and like the role of provider.

I hear bats squeaking in the walls. One flies out of my closet.

My parents meet on my father's leave from the Merchant Marine. My father stands on the beach in shorts and sunglasses.   He must be looking at my mother who holds the camera.   He smiles a quiet smile, not a smile for the camera but at something my mother says or the way she looks.

We were evicted for the second time.   The landlord kept banging on the door most of the night.   We moved in with relatives living in an arboretum on Long Island.   A former Vanderbilt estate stared from across the river.   When I wandered over the grounds, I was on an English country estate surrounded by every type of tree collected from world travels.   The rhododendron hedges were much taller than me. And, it always rained, like it does in England.   The mansion in the arboretum had a gingerbread façade, cross-hatching in shades of brown, the carriage house connected to the house with an archway over the circular drive, the house a museum, now.

Stuffed birds perched on their pedestals,   others ready
        for flight.

A friend is a present you give yourself.

The cot is narrow and rickety. Its metal ends are cold against my skin.   I learn
to sleep on it without thinking about how thin it is,   how I could fall out
at any time.

She is associated with the bounty of the soil.

You will inherit a large sum of money.

Shots fired outside our apartment.   A car on fire.   I wake to a fire engine's
red lights revolving on the walls in my bedroom, my husband asleep beside me.

She guides the vessel's course with a rudder.

The sun came back today. A pine smell rises from the spot where the city burns
Christmas trees,   a blackened circle.

My mother isn't working and lives in a homeless shelter.

The grass grows taller and taller, taking over the yard,   the woman who lives
upstairs puts a red light in her window, her boyfriend beats her.   My mother
disappears for two weeks.   The social worker visits us and talks to my mother,
watching me from the corner of her eye.

The man stretches his hand just beyond the shower curtain and meows like a cat.
My screams echoing beyond the falling water, scare him away. I can clearly see his
hand,   a hard-working, middle-aged hand,   the stubby fingers, the dirt in the
cracks along his palms,   a long life-line.

No one believes me. My aunt turns away from me toward my mother saying, "She
made this up to get attention."

Fortune is light fingered in her ability to take back again; she has many hands.

You can consult her about the future.

At twenty years of age the will reigns; at thirty the wit; at forty the judgment.

He runs his hands along me as I bend over to pick up a leaf. I stand up and turn to confront him, and he is laughing. I can see his hand holding a drink, the ice swirling and melting in a clear liquid, distorting the lines of his palms. He turns and goes back into the kitchen with the other adults.

I'm living in my aunt's house and he is her in-law. If I tell, I see my mother and myself shoved out into the snow drifts.

Working at a library after school, I sometimes take a late school bus home after work. Only a few teenagers are on the bus racing up and down the steep hills formed by a glacier. I walk home down the dark, steep, icy hills. My mother helps me with my homework. She manages to buy Christmas presents and get a Christmas tree every year.

I take my paycheck out of my pocket and put it on the table. My mother hands it back and tells me, "Buy some clothes for yourself."

Your principles mean more to you than any money or success.

The landlady kept coming by the apartment, asking to speak to my mother. My mother told me to wait in the bedroom. They talked about paying the rent and drank coffee my mother served. After a few visits, a notice was tacked onto the door.

The bat clings to the ceiling beam, circles over my bed around and around me, then flies out the bedroom door. The intricate web of pipes is exposed. There isn't a drop ceiling.

You will be traveling and coming into a fortune.

The wind blows up against the corners of the building. I can hear it out the window.

The path runs along a stream covered by a canopy of trees so thick it's difficult to see the sky. Sunlight enters only in patches. I play in certain trees, and on Sundays I fake being too sick to go to church so I can walk through the woods with my father who tells me the names of the plants and trees we pass: willow, birch, oak.

Similarly, fortune catches us on limed twigs, or snares us as if we were birds. We flutter in the air until attracted by the luring branches and then get stuck in the lime. Once captured, she puts her bridle on us.

He plants a garden at the back of the yard. Carrots, squash, scallions, pumpkins, tomatoes, and cucumbers. He weeds and waters for hours. Dirt is ground into the knees of his overalls; a pungent smell reaches me as he stands up. He pulls up carrots and scallions, washing them with the hose, letting me eat them.

My mother comes home early from work, quitting her first job after the divorce. She explains, as she takes off her coat, her scarf, her boots, how she told her new boss the drive to work was too far in the snow. I am eleven and yelling at her.

Your car will be trouble-free for the next 40,000 miles.

The prostitute lives in the basement of our building and has nowhere else to go.

Hanging upside down, she pulls her papery thin wings around herself. She falls asleep in a dark corner, pulsating like a heart.

My grandmother led my mother to a convent that took in homeless girls.   Her sister and brother were sent to a different place.

I dream my mother and I are in a nearly empty house. I'm in what was my room with a box of family photographs. My mother comes into the room and begins to go through the box. I know she'll start ripping them up, so I grab them from her and decide to lock them in my trunk.

People find it difficult to resist your persuasive manner.

In another dream, a high school friend with long red hair is telling me it's time to say good-bye. She's very businesslike about it.

They split the money they get for the house,   and divide up the furniture. Some things stay in the house for the new owners: the piano, dollhouse, an antique sewing machine. The judge agrees each child is worth $100 in support and orders my mother to work.   She has not worked outside the home for twenty years.

And there is no rudder, no crew member at the helm.

There is finally a term for her: displaced homemaker.

As I looked out the picture window, I imagined all our things on the lawn for everyone to see. I pulled out a box and began packing dishes as if I'd done this many times before.   My father showed up the next day to help us move with a truck and his girlfriend.   She was wrapped in a fur coat.

You will participate in a gala affair.

I am looking at the three dresses I can wear to the party and trying to decide which one is the least worn.

Furniture and smaller belongings get left behind during all stages.

The other people in line at the grocery store don't notice we're using food stamps that look almost like money but have the smaller size and papery sound of play money and come in bright colors. Everyone looks annoyed about waiting for the cashier to mark the stamps and then ring up food and nonfood items separately. Welfare will not pay for nonessential items: soap, toilet paper, detergent.   The clerk looks harried as the line grows longer,   she shoves the groceries into bags, turning to the next person.   We pretend not to notice.

I hide beneath the quilt as the bat swings toward me, circling around and around me and diving toward my face.

One learns most when teaching others.

I help her carry the grocery bags through the parking lot, across the highway, then down the tree-lined street.

Good things are being said about you.

I forget about the world surrounding the arboretum,   the highways, feeling shy at school, the clapboard houses and streets where trees have all been cut down. I watch for ghosts near the mansion, the man whose cape is an extension of the way he moves off into the snow. I walk out onto the frozen river.   The snow is really a carpet, the marble mantle over the mahogany fireplace where a fire blazes surrounded by cherry furniture, elegant landscape paintings, portraits of ancestors in long gowns descending the stairs.   You must walk softly here, make little noise if you don't want the house to disappear.

Your mind is creative, original, and alert.

Those cabinet shelves of china will not be passed down to me,   the blue plates with patterns of people harvesting sheaves of wheat.

I wear loosely fitting clothes so no curves show.   I don't talk to boys.

The realtor, wearing a suit, brings a couple and child through the house. The couple exclaim I am the same age as their child, that my room must be a very nice room for a little girl to have. Then they notice the sign I put up about not touching my toys. They move to another part of the house.

Later, my father squats down next to me, and in his soft voice tells me to take down the sign.

Your happiness is intertwined with your outlook on life.

After a while, my friends stop calling me.

She is depicted with a rudder.

The water in the river keeps moving and emptying into the bay. Large houses line the river, boats docked nearby. Geese honk above the trees in the gray sky, in the gray branches.

The furnace keeps turning off in the middle of the night,   snow clings to the windowsills. My mother goes outside in her nightgown, out the front door, around to the back of the house, then down the basement steps to switch it back on.

II
LEAP
Used for effecting horizontal changes in course

The gynecologist and the nurse discuss wallpaper selections for the new office. I feel a pulling high up in my endocervical canal.   The local anesthetic is not working.   I can feel the tissue being looped then yanked from my cervix. It is so painful even a scream isn't possible, as if that were ripped from me, too.

I am not really here in this wallpaperless room.

The infertility and incompetent cervix issues had been discussed.

Judge not according to the appearance.

[79]

It hurts to walk, and I am trying not to cry in the waiting room as I wait for my boyfriend to pick me up. The doctor told me it would be a simple and painless procedure, so I told my boyfriend he didn't need to wait. I wait for him, the ball of pain widening as a pregnant woman stares at me, and the women on the health channel chatter at us from the large-screen TV.

Your efforts are budding.

The uterus itself is anteverted and firm without palpable adnexal masses or tenderness. Actually, fairly normal in appearance, a little ectropion, consistent possibly from where the recent Loop Electrosurgical Encision Procedure (LEEP) was done, but not as distorted as I might have thought.

You will have good luck in your personal affairs.

I am staring at the poster on the ceiling. Another doctor comes into the room and heads to where my legs are apart. He is here to observe the procedure. I am not numb enough.

There are many new opportunities that are being presented to you.

Fortune's house is often on a towering rock.

Abnormal cells are present in this specimen and are consistent with mild dysplasia. Red blood cells present. Endocervical cells present.

Return in six months following the pap if this one is normal.

The waiting room could be some woman's room, pink wallpaper, baskets of fake flowers, women's magazines. The cervix is pink.

[80]

You must learn day-by-day to broaden your horizon.

Her worldly possessions rest on a shaky foundation and are exposed to the winds of adversity, which naturally she could suffer.

I had to go somewhere else. It gets easier.   It hurts to have sex.   I'm afraid it will hurt every time.   I am not supposed to ask questions about what will happen.

Endo/Exocervical component.

You may attend a party where strange customs prevail.

No show for follow-up pap.

We did find abnormalities on your recent pap smear. You should consult your doctor concerning the significance of these abnormalities and what further investigation or treatment he would advise.

End of report.

III

ATLANTIC CITY

A large sum of money

Fortuna bears a cornucopia as the giver of abundance and a rudder as controller of destinies or stands on a ball to indicate the uncertainty of fortune. A capricious dispenser of good and ill fortune.

In Caesar's Palace the slot machines whir and clang all along the ballroom floor, huge crystal chandeliers above. My mother has an uncanny way of finding the ones that give money.

Among her monuments was a temple at Argos, where the legendary Palamedes is said to have dedicated to her the first set of dice, which he is supposed to have invented.

Sometimes her eyes appear, and very expressively, as when one of them weeps and the other laughs.

A colonnade of plaster Romans circle us as we take a snapshot outside the casino. They gesture toward the flat golden doors—

Caesar welcomes us over the loudspeaker,

"Come this way."

Drug deals are going on as I walk up the steps of the shelter to see my mother. It's warm, humid, the salt smells of the ocean mingled with cigarette smoke. My mother peers out of her room before coming out. For a second, I glimpse a single light bulb hanging from a ceiling, an unmade bed, some plastic grocery bags. A stray cat follows us down the long hallway.

Her frailty is like glass. Her face may smile, but she stings just the same, and resembles a serpent or (even better) a scorpion.

There is a long wait for the elevator. Elderly people wait on walkers, lean on canes, sit in wheelchairs.

Walk through life with a good heart, and you will run with success.

Originally a farming deity, she eventually represented luck. She came to be identified with Tyche, the patroness of cities and goddess of fortune among the Hellenistic Greeks.

A bat   boomeranging beneath a street lamp   swooping

to grab a moth or insect.

The method could be simple, such as the casting of lots or the rustling of tree leaves, or more sophisticated, taking the form of a direct inquiry of an inspired person who then

[82]

gave the answer orally. One of the most common methods was incubation, in which the inquirer slept in a holy precinct and received an answer in a dream. Oracles delivered through incubation were believed to come from underworld powers.

Consultants slept on skins.

She took off her wings and shoes, since she intended to remain there.

I invoke you here.

He who has imagination without learning has wings but no feet.

My sister's old apartment building on the boardwalk has been turned into a haunted house. I used to walk her dog here, along the beach, the dog disappearing in and out of the early morning fog, running into waves of fog, waves of ocean.

No mere "Lady Luck," she was the energy that drove men and women to reproduce themselves. Fortuna was originally "she who brings," the goddess who permitted the fertilization of humans, animals, and plants; thus she was worshipped by women desiring pregnancy and gardeners seeking bumper crops. The goddess who made women irresistible to men, who was worshipped by a regular invasion of the men's public baths by luck-seeking Roman women.

Someone runs yelling up the stairs.

We go to a casino buffet for dinner. An abundance of food is everywhere, a whole dessert bar, fruit bar, but my mother's face is drawn and thin, and her impulse is still to mother me and tell me to eat more. A cornucopia spills fake flowers, fake fruit.

For better luck you have to wait 'til autumn.

IV
Good Fortune

One who has good fortune, especially a
wealthy person. A person's condition or
standing in life determined by material
possessions or financial wealth.

I pass by the photographs of other women who went to this college in the nineteenth century. In one photo, rows and rows of women study together underneath candles at long tables. In another photo, they wander over these same brick paths through campus.

In the dream, the empty house expresses her presence   scrapes on the walls revealed by the furniture taken out, spots on the carpet, peeling paint, odd-shaped rooms, scraped floors.

You will never need to worry about a steady income.

Milk
        heavy
                in the yellow glass.

𝔥uman dignity, then, consisted not in the exercise of will to shape destiny but in the use of reason to contemplate and perhaps to tolerate fate.

My dream   wandering around the hotel by myself,   a huge, square building. I follow the hallways until I find some empty rooms that are unlocked. I go inside and can hear the ocean even before I finish opening the doors and entering the rooms. I feel a sudden sense of being home. I should be here, but the room isn't vacant and belongs to someone else, and I am trespassing.

There is no cosmetic for beauty like happiness.

I'm put on a waiting list to get into a college creative writing class, but one of the poets teaching the class agrees to work with me over a January term. His mobile of birds

[84]

spins above us as he goes over my poems.　　　The campus is deserted, snow covered, and under drifts as I curl up in the library with huge windows, reading poetry.

Red-haired twin sisters room together, and they both write poetry, order pizzas from their room, ride horses, their long red hair, streaks of fire.　　　They sit across from me in my first creative writing class.　　　My roommate keeps her cello in our room sleeping in its case between our beds, riding in a seat next to her on the plane home.

Not knowing certain things in graduate school: how to talk during receptions, how to stand in elegant rooms with chandeliers, how to stand on balconies, how to make small talk, how to find a voice in the classroom, how to be certain I have ideas worth listening to, how not to look too rumpled after riding the bus to get there.

Everyone at the table is describing trips abroad.

The futon is on the floor.　　The carpet is old, dirty, smelly.　　Drinks have been spilled on it, and cigarette holes are burned in.　　The futon is cold.　　I drink my roommate's milk since I am out of food and money.

Bats are symbols of good luck.

V
CARRIED OVER THE THRESHOLD

> Fortuna had a following of married women
> who asked her to preserve their sex appeal
> so they could keep their husbands happy.

Tubes tethered to every part of my husband, parts taken from his body.　A window looks out on a glassed-in corridor that's being built.　Trash and debris scattered below the scaffolding,　　　beyond it hills, trees, a lake hidden there.　I drive there after work for three days, the days like an obstacle course to get through to see him.　If one section is taken out, does it all collapse?

The apartment has a fireplace,　　　tile around the fireplace, a mantle.　　　A stand of trees gathered outside the windows.　　　The cottonwood is familiar, her sequined gown. I remember her. The cat sits puffed up and purring by the fireplace.

I stand at his head and stroke his hair. A gesture, but still the right one, the only one. The bed, more like a machine with wires and tubes to handle every bodily fluid, taking up the whole room. I am here with him and watching the sky pinking up, watching him sleep.

Invoked by newly married women who dedicated their virgin garments in her temples.

In this long, black, crinkled broom-skirt, see-through, the skirt pulled up around me, legs apart, like a bat or some creature.

You are the guiding star of his existence.

The cat's eyes have lines in them—they look like maps.

The goddess was queen of the household.

Staring into the branches of the tree outside our apartment or into my closet.

A huge painting, a portrait of a lady in blue, floats in a small boat and sinks into the water.

Storms,   the worst ones packing 100-mph winds, and I feel helpless about what to do, put the cat in her carrier, stand near the windows,   the worst thing to do,   reports of a tornado setting down nearby.

The night life is for you.

Blown here: my room with painted desk, whirls of energetic paint, green, black, gold splattered, blown here, then suddenly it's quiet,   solid furniture, walls,

[86]

hallway, balcony, fireplace, cat, husband, Matisse with fish in a glass of water, green leaves blowing in a breeze, hearth, verandah, grounds, wind, train whistles, owl almost sounding like a person somewhere above the roof at two a.m.,   silence before and after, a two-syllable sound   who-whoo   over the apartment, more like a word and a human voice than any other animal sound I've heard, but suspended in the air above me, around me, the cat and I listening.

As he turns and sighs in his sleep, he sounds like a breeze picking up for a moment in a tree outside the window.

VI
ALL ROADS LEAD TO HOME

> The place where one resides. A family liv-
> ing in a dwelling. A place of origin. A
> headquarters. An objective or place of
> safety in some games. To the center or
> heart of something.

The taxi from the Rome airport swerves around a rocky hill. We can see Fortuna's white temple rising above the cypress.

In Italy Fortuna was consulted even by the Roman emperors. Her worship in Rome was introduced by the king most favored by Fortuna, even to the point of physical relationship.

After I finish my doctorate, I get rejection letters for teaching jobs with hundreds of qualified applicants.

Simplicity and clarity should be your theme in dress.

Interview: me in cranberry suits, black suits, navy suits.

A fashion show, models strutting down the Spanish Steps, statues of the muses gath-
ered around ancient lily ponds, the movement of their drapery stopped, a hint of flesh, hip, curving underneath.

Mussolini's highway is constructed over the ruins.

We may follow her, she may intercept our paths, she may flee from us.

Fragments: heads, columns, a giant foot. Plants in urns, cool marble steps in July.

At an interview for a non-teaching job, the interviewer wants to know what my career goals are, why I'm applying for this job since I'm so overqualified.

Walking the narrow, winding streets to get gelato at night, people telling fortunes in the piazza, picking pockets, a struggle between man and beast carved into a fountain in the middle of all this, a language like water that flows from people without hesitation or correction.

The young girl at the shelter where I work comes into my office to hide from the noise. She likes to read, make up stories for me about butterflies. We play Clue together.

Her light brown hair falls forward, a curtain around her face. For the first time, she expresses grief over losing her mother, a waterfall that looks like it has no end. I sit beside her in the waiting room at the shelter.

Fortune makes sure of her prey by catching her victim in a net. We are symbolized as fish struggling in the weltering sea of life and finally caught by the goddess.

We all sit around the table eating breakfast at the shelter for teenagers. I like these meals at my job here. Around me the teenagers' faces and the faces of my co-workers. One boy still has baby fat in his cheeks, round, red cheeks. A social worker found him abandoned in an empty house without food, electricity, heat, running water. For this moment, we have everything: pancakes, syrup, orange juice, cereal, milk, eggs, bacon. A warm house holding out the sleet. Even though the boy looks like a child, he is large and sometimes doesn't know his own strength as he throws a chair, a TV at one of the workers. Today he is calm.

Brand-new white and beige bedding and furniture, light walls,   very little color, sheer curtains,   huge windows and the shoreline below, the constant, crashing waves, the sea colors, non-colors, a feeling of open spaces and light. I want to stand here looking out the windows and hearing only the sound of the ocean not the noise of city life.

[88]

Nuns singing out of tune in the Basilica of St. Cecilia.   Her image carved on a marble casket,   her hair flowing over her face, her limp body beneath the folds of her dress.

I put the rejection letters and applications away and teach where and when I can, for the chance to see the people in the room writing,   swarming and circling the Art Deco lamps and steeples,   high-pitched echolocating off objects near them, sounds, words,   guides through   the night-sky.

She was generally represented as blind.

Chic women steer their scooters around traffic jams, men talk on their cell-phones, passing swiftly beneath her temple rising above them, unseen.

I startle a huge heron as I ride my bike. She glides over the ditch running alongside the road. She has a gray wingspan and long neck. How could something that long necked and huge fly so gracefully and silently? She flies beside me effortlessly.

Suzette Marie Bishop teaches at Texas A&M International University in Laredo, Texas. She received her B.A. from Oberlin College, her M.F.A. from the University of Virginia, and her D.A. from the State University of New York at Albany. Her poems have appeared in numerous journals, including *The Antioch Review*, *Aries*, *13th Moon*, and *The Little Magazine*, and in an anthology, *The Virago Book of Birth Poetry*. One of her poems won *The Spoon River Poetry Review* Editors' Prize, and she published a chapbook, *Cold Knife Surgery*. She lives in Laredo with her husband and her Siamese cat, Zippy.

THE MAY SWENSON
POETRY AWARD

This annual competition, named for May Swenson, honors her as one of America's most provocative, insouciant, and vital poets. In John Hollander's words, she was "one of our few unquestionably major poets." During her long career, May was loved and praised by writers from virtually every major school of poetry. She left a legacy of nearly fifty years of writing when she died in 1989.

May Swenson lived most of her adult life in New York City, the center of poetry writing and publishing in her day. But she is buried in Logan, Utah, her birthplace and hometown.